I0158587

Freedom from Self

Guidance for Christian Living

François Fénelon

REJUVENATED BOOKS

Series One

Freedom from Self
Rejuvenated Books: Series One
ISBN: 978-1-63171-002-5

About this text: François de Salignac de La Mothe-Fénelon was a French archbishop and man of letters whose writings had broad impact on French culture and religion in the seventeenth and eighteenth centuries. His correspondence also provided spiritual guidance to many Christians of the day. The advice presented in this book was originally published in French as *Avis Chrestien*. We have excerpted, arranged, and paraphrased his words from an elderly English translation that was published as the first section of this volume:

Fénelon, François and Madame Guyon. *Spiritual Progress: or Instructions in the Divine Life of the Soul.* Edited by James W. Metcalf. New York: M. W. Dodd, 1853.

This book is printed in the United States of America.

Contents

THIS IS THE WHOLE of religion — to move out of the self and self-love in order to move into God.

ONE

The Knowledge of God

What Christians lack most is God. They've learned that history records certain miracles and acts of providence. They've reflected upon the corruption and instability of the world. They may even be convinced that reshaping their lives according to certain moral principles is necessary to be right with God. However, the whole of this building lacks a foundation. This pious exterior has no soul. The life that enlivens every believer—God himself, the all and in all, the author and king of all things—is missing.

It isn't astonishing that Christians do so little for God and that the little they do is so costly in their minds. They don't know him. They barely believe that he exists. The impression they have of God is more a blind deference for public opinion rather than a living belief in him. They assume he must exist because they lack the courage to examine the matter and because they are indifferent. Their souls are distracted by their desires for other objects. They think of God as a stern and powerful being who is forever making demands on them, thwarting their desires, and threatening them with great punishment. These are the thoughts of those who take religion seriously, and even their number is small enough. "God is love," says John. Anyone who doesn't love him doesn't know him, for how could anyone know love without loving it? It is plain, then, that those who have only feared God have not yet known him.

My God, you do everything, but the world does not see you. I myself wandered everywhere in vain, searching for you outside of myself. I considered the wonders of nature to form some idea of your greatness. I asked your creatures about you. I never once thought I might find you in the depths of my heart, where you had never ceased to dwell. No, my God, it isn't necessary to descend into the depths or travel over the seas or rise up into the heavens to find you. You are closer to me than I am to myself. However, when I tell people to look for you in their own hearts, it's like I've told them to search for you in the farthest unknown lands.

What land is more distant and unknown to the great majority of them, vain and self-indulgent as they are, as the ground of their own heart? Do they ever understand what it means to enter into themselves? Have they ever tried to find the way? Can they even form the faintest idea of the nature of that inner sanctuary, that impenetrable depth of the soul where you desire to be worshiped in spirit and in truth? They're always outside of themselves, focused on the objects of their ambition or their pleasure. If they don't understand what it means to come into themselves through serious reflection, what will they say if they're asked to come out of themselves in order to be lost in God?

As for me, my creator, I close my eyes to all outward things, which are nothing more than "vanity and a striving after wind," so that in the deepest parts of my heart, I may enjoy an intimate companionship with you through Jesus Christ your son, who is your wisdom and eternal understanding. He became a child so that though his life and the foolishness of his cross, he would put to shame my vain and lying wisdom. Whatever the cost, and in spite of my fears and conjecture, I want to be lowly, a fool, more despised in my own eyes than in the eyes of the worldly wise and their way of thinking. Like the apostles, I want to become drunk with the Holy Spirit and with them become a joke in this world.

When I am good, it's because you make me so. No only do you guide my heart as you please, but you give me a heart like yours. You are the life of my soul just as my soul is the life of my body. You are more intimately present to me than I am to myself. This "I," to which I am so attached and which I have loved so fiercely, should be foreign to me in comparison with you. You are the one who gave it to me. Without you, it would never have existed. Therefore, it is your desire that I should love you better than I love it.

My God, in those souls that draw back from your pure love, I see the darkness and rebellion resulting of the fall. The scriptures teach that the goodness of the creatures you created had no claim upon themselves but acknowledged that they belonged to their creator. Father, your children are sadly changed. They no longer look like you. They want to reverse this holy pattern, madly lifting up themselves as gods. They want to belong only to themselves, to do everything for the self, or at the very least, to surrender themselves to you with exceptions and conditions and only for their own advantage.

My God, you are at once so great and so humble, so high above the heavens and so available to your creatures in their misery, so infinite and so intimately enclosed in the depths of my heart, so terrifying and so lovely, so jealous and so open to requests from those who talk to you with the familiarity of pure love. When will your children cease to be ignorant of you? Where will I find a voice loud enough to rebuke the whole world for its blindness and with authority tell it everything that you are?

I leave myself, Father, in your hands. Make and remake this clay. Shape it or grind it into dust. It is yours alone. May it always serve your eternally blessed plans. Let nothing in me oppose the goodness for which I was created. Require, command, forbid—what do you want me to do? What should I not do? Honored or humbled, rejoicing or suffering, doing your work or set aside, I will praise you just the same, yielding all of my own will to yours. Nothing remains for me but to adopt the words of Mary: "May it be done to me according to your word."

Two

The Death of Self

Scarcely anyone who desires to serve God does so for unselfish reasons. People expect gain and not loss, consolation and not suffering, riches and not poverty, expansion and not contraction. However, the work of God is opposite in nature. It is the work of being lost, sacrificed, made less than nothing, and stripped of pleasure—even pleasure in the gifts of God—so that you are forced to cling only to him.

In the beginning, God gradually takes away the things that you love too much and in opposition to his law. But although this outer work is essential in laying the foundation of the building, it only goes so far toward completing the entire structure. After God has stripped you and dead-ened your flesh toward the created things to which it clung, there comes a time when he begins an inner work to force you away from your hold on the self. He wants to tear away the I, the center of your self-love, for it was only for the sake of this I that you loved all the rest. Trim up the branches of a tree, and far from killing it, you increase its liveliness. It sends shoots out again on every side. However, if you attack the trunk and roots, it fades, languishes, and dies. This is the will of God for you, to make you die to self.

God reserves for his own hand the work of attacking the soul in its depths, of taking away the last traces of the life of self. The strength of the soul is no longer used against outward things. Instead, the weakness of the soul is turned against itself. The soul looks at the self and is shocked at what it sees. It remains faithful but no longer sees its own faithfulness. Every defect from its past now rises up to be seen—and often with new faults that it never suspected. It no longer finds comfort from the passion and courage that used to feed it. It faints. Like Jesus, it is weary even to death. God strips the self away, little by little, removing all of the clothing in which the soul is wrapped, piece by piece. These last works are not always the greatest works, but they are the most severe.

God never leaves the soul until he has made it supple and pliable by twisting it all manner of ways. At one time, you must speak frankly. At another time, you must be still. You must be praised, then blamed, then forgotten, and then examined again. You must suffer condemnation without saying a word in self-defense, and then later, you must speak well of yourself. You must be willing to find yourself dried out, languishing, weary of God, intellectually exhausted, so far removed from every gracious thought that you're tempted to despair. These are examples of some of the plundering that now desolates you, but there are endless others that God sends according to his own wise purposes.

Don't tell me that this is idle imagination. Can anyone doubt that God works directly in the soul? That he acts to make the soul die to self? That, after conquering the baser desires, he attacks all the crafty, inner reserves of self-love — especially in those souls that have generously and unreservedly given themselves up to the working of his grace? The more he desires to purify them, the more he works within them. The world doesn't have the eyes to see or the ears to hear these trials, but the world is blind. Its wisdom is dead. It cannot coexist with the Spirit of truth. "No one knows the thoughts of God except the Spirit of God," says the apostle. "The Spirit searches all things, even the deep things of God."

At first, you aren't comfortable with this inner guidance that tends to tear you down to the foundation. You may be willing to be silent and reflective, but you don't want to risk listening to the inner voice that calls you to the sacrifices that God prepares. You're like the child Samuel, who didn't yet know the Lord. When the Lord called, he thought it was Eli, and Eli told him that he had been dreaming, that no one had spoken to him. In the same way, you're unsure whether that voice might be something you imagined that will carry you too far. Your spiritual advisers may tell you that you've been dreaming and urge you to go back to bed. However, God continues to wake you until you listen to what he has to say.

Yielding to this guidance is how souls make great strides forward. Those who are childlike enough to never hesitate soon make amazing progress. Others argue, never failing to find reasons to not follow the inner guide. They are willing but not willing. They want to wait for certainty. They look for advisers who will tell them to not do what they are afraid of doing. They stop at every step and look back, languishing in indecision, and gradually reject the Spirit of God. At first, they grieve him with hesitation. Then they irritate him with formal resistance. In the end, they extinguish his workings with repeated opposition. While

11

they resist the Spirit in this way, they find pretexts to hide and justify their resistance, but they gradually dry out. They lose their simplicity, and no matter what they do to deceive themselves, they are not at peace. At the bottom of the conscience, there is a sense of reproach that they have been lacking in their dedication to God.

As God becomes more distant — because *they* are leaving *him* — the soul becomes hardened by degrees. It's no longer peaceful, and it no longer seeks true peace. On the contrary, it wanders farther and farther from peace by looking for peace where peace cannot be found. The soul becomes like a dislocated bone, a continual source of pain and out of its natural position, but in spite of that, it shows no tendency to return to its natural place. Instead, it binds itself securely to its false location.

In the sacrifice that you make when you devote yourself entirely to God, you hold nothing back and feel good about that, too, while looking at things in general and at a distance. However, when God takes you at your word and accepts your offer in detail, he shows you a thousand repulsive things whose existence you hadn't even suspected. Your courage then fails. You flatter your feeble and tempted soul with frivolous excuses. You only do half of what God requires, mixing the guidance of God with that of the self, trying to find some food for that corrupt interior that doesn't want to die. Your jealous God retreats from you. The soul begins to close its eyes so that it won't see that it's lost the courage to act. God leaves the soul to its weakness and corruption because the soul wants to be left so. But think about the magnitude of this error!

God has spared nothing to own you entirely. He has become the inward bridegroom who takes great care in doing everything for his bride—but he is infinitely jealous. Don't be surprised at the demanding nature of his jealousy. What does it demand? Is it talents, enlightenment, the regular practice of outward virtues? Not at all. God is relaxed and forgiving in all such matters. Love is only jealous about love. All of God's scrutiny falls upon the condition of the will. He can't share the heart of his bride with any other. Even less can he tolerate the excuses by which she would convince herself that the division of her heart is justified. The moment that you refuse anything that God asks and begin to deceive yourself in that refusal, God begins to consider you, in that same moment, to be an unfaithful wife—and one who tries to conceal her infidelity. If you cling to any small thing, however good it may appear, he arrives, sword in hand, to cut into the deepest corner of the soul. If you are still fearful in any hidden place, he goes to that spot because he always attacks you at your weakest points.

Poor soul, so weak in spirit! How these final blows overwhelm you! The very apprehension of them makes you tremble and retreat. So few manage to cross this fearful desert. Scarcely two or three are able to reach the Promised Land. Woe to those who resist the inner guidance, who sin against the Holy Spirit. Those who resist the Spirit while striving for their salvation will be punished in this world by affliction and in the next world by the pains of hell. Happy are those who never hesitate, who only fear that they follow the Spirit with too little readiness, who would rather do too much against the self than do too little.

At length, when the soul no longer hesitates to lose all and forget self, it possesses everything. This is not a conscious possession, so that the soul looks upon itself as happy, for that would be a return to self after leaving it forever. It is instead a likeness to the state of those in heaven who are forever enraptured by the contemplation of God—without having a moment, during the whole of eternity, to think about themselves and their happiness. They are so satisfied in these joys that they rejoice eternally without ever saying to themselves that they are happy.

O bridegroom of souls, you give freely to the souls who never resist you! Even in this life, you give them a foretaste of that happiness.

Freedom from Self

Unrestrained by any attachment to created things or any thought of self, these souls enter into your own immensity. Nothing holds them back. They become continually more and more lost in you. They are always satisfied. They do not possess happiness, but their happiness possesses them. Ask them at any moment, "Do you desire to have what you lack?" Without hesitation, they will answer, "I desire to lack what I lack. I desire everything that God desires. I want nothing else."

These are those who worship in spirit and in truth. You seek such as these to worship you, but you rarely find them. Most try to guide you instead of being guided by you. They give themselves up to you so that they will become great, but they withdraw from you when you require them to be little. O God, your creatures do not know for what purpose you have made them. Teach them. In the depths of their souls, write that the clay must allow itself to be shaped as the potter desires.

THREE

Self-Abandonment

To abandonment your self means to value your self as worth nothing. Anyone who has perceived the difficulty of doing this has learned the meaning of this self-renunciation that so offends human nature. The source of the trouble is that people love themselves with a blind passion that amounts to idolatry. If they love anything beyond themselves, it is only for their own sake.

You must not deceive yourself regarding those friendships in which it appears as though you forget yourself so much that you only think about the interests of your friends. In these friendships that appear — both to yourself and to the world — to be so generous and disinterested, you seek the pleasure of loving without repayment. Even though you don't desire to be served by your friends, you desire to be loved by them. You hope that they will be charmed with what you do for them without expecting anything in return. In this way, you get the same reward that you seem to despise, for what is more delicious to a subtle self-love than to hear itself praised for not being self-love? Self-love finds no glory equal to that of appearing to seek nothing at all.

However, it's not difficult to unmask this pride that appears to be no pride at all. If those whom it loves fail to repay it with friendship, respect, and confidence, it is mortally wounded. It's then easy to see that it isn't disinterested, though it tries so hard to appear so. It may not seek lifeless praise, money, or dignity. Nevertheless, it must be paid. It's greedy for the respect of good people. It loves so that it will be loved in return and admired for its disinterestedness. It seems to forget self so that, by that means, it draws the attention of the whole world upon self alone.

It does not, indeed, make all these reflections in detail. It does not say, in so many words, "I will deceive the whole world with my generosity so that the world will love and admire me." No, it would never dare to apply such base and unworthy language to itself. It deceives itself along with the rest of the world. It admires itself for its generosity in the same way that a beautiful woman admires her beauty in a mirror. It is moved by seeing that it is more generous and more disinterested than the rest of humankind. The illusion that it presents to others extends to itself. It passes off upon itself the same thing that it passes off upon others — generosity — and this is what pleases it more than anything else.

Nothing will close your heart to the grace of self-abandonment as much as self-love that is disguised as worldly generosity. You should be especially wary of it because of your natural disposition towards it. The greater your natural gifts for frankness, disinterestedness, pleasure in doing good, love of honor, and generous friendship, the more actively must you distrust your self and be wary of placing your confidence in these natural gifts. Only the love of God can make you come out of self. If his powerful hand did not help you, you wouldn't know how to take the first step in that direction.

God does two things, and only he has the power to do them. First, he reveals himself to you, with all his rights over the creature and with all the charm of his goodness. You then see that because you have not made yourself, you are not made for yourself but are created for the glory of him whose pleasure it was to make you. You see that he is too great to make anything except for himself, and that your satisfaction and happiness must therefore come from losing yourself in him. No created thing, however dazzling it may be, can make you realize this in relation to itself. Far from finding in created things this infinity that so fills you and carries you away from yourself in God, you discover in created things only emptiness, a powerlessness to fill your heart, an imperfection that continually drives you into yourself.

The second miracle that God performs is to do what he pleases within your heart after he has enlightened your understanding. He isn't satisfied with presenting his own delightful characteristics. He also makes you love him by producing his love within your heart. He himself creates within you the love that he shows you is owed to him.

You desire, perhaps, to know more in detail what this self-abandonment consists of. I will try to satisfy you.

There is little difficulty in understanding that you must reject criminal pleasures, unjust gains, and base vanities. Renouncing these things consists of a contempt that repudiates them absolutely and forbids you from deriving any enjoyment from them. However, it's not so easy to understand that you must also abandon property that is honestly acquired, the enjoyment of a modest and well-spent life, the honors that come

21

from a good reputation, and virtue that raises you above the reach of envy.

The reason that you don't understand why these things must be given up is that you aren't required to discard them with disgust. On the contrary, you must preserve them for use in whatever station divine providence places you. You must make sober use of them—but without desiring to enjoy them or setting your heart on them. I say "sober use of them" because when you're not attached to a thing for the sake of self-enjoyment and of seeking happiness in it, you only use as much of it as you need to. You can see this in wise and faithful stewards who are careful to only use as much of their masters' property as is precisely required to meet their needs.

Jesus said, "Those of you who do not give up everything you have cannot be my disciples." It follows that Christians must abandon everything they have, however innocent, because if they don't renounce it, it ceases to be innocent. They must abandon those things that they must also guard with the greatest possible care—the welfare of their families or their own reputations—because they must not set their hearts on any of these things. They are to love these others for God only, to make sober use of the comforts of friendship so that their needs may be met, to be ready to part with their loved ones whenever God wills it, and never to seek in their loved ones the true resting place for their hearts.

That is the purity of true Christian friendship. It only seeks the heavenly spouse in the mortal and earthly friend. In this way, you make use of the world and its creature without abusing them, as Paul writes in 1 Corinthians 7. You do not desire to find pleasure in them. You only use what God gives you, what he desires that you should love, and you accept it without giving away your heart. It is in this sense that Christ wants you to leave father and mother, brothers and sisters, and friends. It is in this sense that he "did not come to bring peace, but a sword." God is a jealous God. If, in the recesses of your soul, you are attached to any creature, your heart is not worthy of him. He must reject your heart like a spouse who divides her affections between her bridegroom and a stranger.

Having abandoned all outward things that are not self, it still remains for you to complete the sacrifice by abandoning all inward things, including the self. Renouncing the body is fearful to most sensitive and worldly-minded persons. They know nothing that is more themselves than this body, which they flatter and adorn with so much care. Even when they're deprived of its graces, they often maintain a love for its life that amounts to a shameful cowardice. Even the word "death" makes them shudder. If your natural courage raises you above these fears, you may say, "I don't desire to flatter my body, nor to hesitate in accepting its destruction whenever God decides to weaken it and destroy it into ashes." You may thus renounce the body, but in renouncing the spirit, great obstacles may still block the way.

You have the same feelings for your under-standing, your wisdom, and your virtue that a young and worldly woman has for her beauty. You take pleasure in them. It gives you a satis-faction to feel that you are wise, sober, and safe from the impulses that you see in others. You are intoxicated with the pleasure of not being intox-icated with pleasure. You renounce with coura-geous restraint the most flattering temptations of the world, and then you content yourself with the satisfaction that comes from this proof of your self-control. What subtle poison! How unfaithful you are to God when you give your heart to this refined self-love. You must renounce all self-satisfaction and all natural contentment in your own wisdom and virtue.

Remember that the more pure and elevated God's gifts are, the more God is jealous of them. He showed mercy to the first human rebel, but he denied it to the angels. Both sinned out of self-love, but because the angel was perfect and regarded as a sort of divinity, God punished his unfaithfulness with a fiercer jealousy than he did man's disobedience. You can infer from this that God is more jealous of his most excellent gifts than he is of the more common ones. He wants you to be attached to nothing but himself and to consider his gifts, however excellent, as nothing but a way for you to be more easily and intimately attached to him. Whoever considers the grace of God with self-satisfaction — with a kind pleasure in ownership — turns that grace into poison.

Therefore, live, as it were, on trust. All that is in you and all that you are is only loaned you. Use it according to the will of the one who lends it, and never for a moment think of it as your own. This is true self-abandonment. It's not accomplished through painful reflections and struggles. God himself will take you by the hand and guide you in self-renunciation through every moment of every day. It's only when you refrain from self-contemplation and trying to master yourself in your own way that you lose yourself in God.

FOUR

The Holy Spirit

It's clear from the holy scriptures that the Spirit of God lives within you. He works there, praying without ceasing, groaning, desiring, asking on your behalf for what you don't know how to ask for yourself. He urges you on, enlivens you, speaks to you when you're silent, and suggests all truth to you. He so unites you to God that you become one spirit with God.

This is the teaching of faith, and even those teachers who are farthest from the inward life can't help but acknowledge it. However, in spite of those principles, these teachers forever labor to assert that it is the outward law, or at least the light of learning and reason, that inwardly illuminates

27

you. They teach that your understanding acts on its own based on that instruction. These teachers don't sufficiently rely upon the inward teacher, the Holy Spirit, who does everything within you. He is the soul of your soul. You couldn't form a thought or desire without him. What blindness you have! You think that you're alone in the inner sanctuary when God is much more intimately present there than even you are.

"What do you mean?" you might ask. "Are all Christians inspired?"

Yes! They are all undoubtedly inspired. They're not inspired like the prophets and apostles, but without the actual inspiration of the Spirit of grace, they could neither do, nor desire, nor believe any good thing. They are always inspired, but they always stifle that inspiration. God never stops speaking to them, but the noise of their outward lives and inward passions shuts them off from him and prevents their hearing.

You must silence everything—including the self—so that in the deep stillness of the soul you can perceive the indescribable voice of the bridegroom. You must lend an attentive ear, for his voice is soft and still. It's only heard by those who hear nothing else. How rare it is to find a soul that's quiet enough to hear God speak. The slightest murmur of your vanities—or of love that's fixed upon self—confounds all the words of the Spirit of God. You hear clearly enough that he's speaking and that he's asking for something, but you can't distinguish what he says, and you're often glad enough that you can't. The smallest holding back, the slightest self-reflection, the most imperceptible fear of hearing too clearly what God demands will interfere with the inner voice.

Should you be astonished, then, that so many people—truly religious people but people who are also in love with entertainment, vain desires, false wisdom, and confidence in their own virtues—cannot hear his voice and consider its existence to be the dream of fanatics? What will they do with their proud reasoning? How effective will the words of pastors or even of the scriptures themselves be if they do not have the Holy Spirit within them, giving life to the words of others? The outward word — even the gospel — becomes an empty sound without the fertile, enlivening, inner word: "For the letter alone kills, but the Spirit gives life."

Eternal and omnipotent Word of the Father! You are the one who speaks in the depth of your children's souls. The words that came from the mouth of the savior only have the power to produce such miraculous fruit because they're enlivened by that Spirit of life that is the Word itself. This is why Peter says, "Lord, to whom would you go? You have the words of eternal life."

It's not just the outward law of the gospel that God shows you inwardly through the light of reason and faith. It is his very Spirit that speaks, touches, enlivens, and works within you. The Spirit does within you and with you whatever you do that is good, just as the soul gives life to the body and governs all its actions.

Therefore, you truly are continually inspired. You do not lead a grace-filled life except as you act under this inner inspiration. O God, how few Christians sense that inspiration! Only a few do not annihilate it with their voluntary distractions or their resistance.

God speaks within the unrepentant, too, but stupefied as they are by the noise of the world and their desires, they cannot hear him. To them, the inner voice is a fable.

God also speaks within wise and enlightened people whose outwardly proper lives appear to be clothed with many virtues, but these are often too full of themselves and their own ideas to listen to God. Everything is turned into reasoning. They exchange the principles of human wisdom and the plans of good judgment for the truth that would flow infinitely better through the channel of simple, willing openness to the word of God. They appear to be good people, sometimes better than others. They are so, perhaps, to a certain point. However, it is a mixed goodness.

31

They remain in possession of themselves—and desire always to be so—according to the boundaries of their reason. They love to be guided by their own counsel and to be strong and powerful in their own eyes.

When God speaks within awakened sinners, they sense the deep regrets of conscience, which is the voice of God reproaching them inwardly for their sins. When they are deeply moved, they have no trouble understanding this inward voice because it's the voice that pierces them so sharply. That voice within them is the two-edged sword that Paul says "penetrates even to dividing soul and spirit." God makes himself perceived, enjoyed, and followed. They hear the sweet voice that buries a reproach in the bottom of the heart and tears the heart into pieces. This is true and pure contrition.

I thank you, my God, that you have hidden your inexpressible secrets from these great and wise ones and have delighted in revealing them to weak and humble souls. Only with little children are you wholly unreserved. You treat everyone else in their own manner. They desire knowledge and great virtues, so you give them dazzling illuminations and turn them into heroes. But this is not the better part. You hide something greater for your dearest children. They lie at your breast with John. As for the great ones who constantly fear having to stoop or be humbled, you leave them to their greatness. They will never share your gentle touches and closeness because to deserve that, they would have to become like little children and play at your knees.

I have often observed that a common, ignorant sinner who is just beginning to be touched by a living awareness of God's love is much more likely to listen to this inward language of the Spirit of grace than enlightened and learned people who have grown old in their own wisdom. God's one desire is to communicate himself, but he cannot, so to speak, find a place to set his foot in souls that are so full of themselves, that have grown fat upon their own wisdom and virtues. As the scripture says, "his secret is with the simple."

Where are they? I do not find them. God himself sees them and loves to live in them. "My Father and I," Jesus says, "will come to them and make your home with them." A soul that is rescued from self and abandoned to grace, that considers itself to be nothing, and that follows without thought the will of that pure love that is its perfect guide — that soul has an experience that the wise can neither receive nor understand.

I was once as wise as any other. Thinking I saw everything, I saw nothing. I crept along, feeling my way forward through a succession of reasonings, but there was no ray to enlighten my darkness. I was content to reason. But when you have silenced everything within so that you may listen to God, you know all things without knowing anything. Then you see that you were utterly ignorant of all that you thought you understood. You lose everything that you once had, and you don't care. You have nothing then that belongs to self. Everything is lost, and you are lost with it. Something within you joins the bridegroom in singing, "Show me your face, let me hear your voice, for your voice is sweet, and your face is lovely." Oh, how sweet that voice is! How it makes me tremble within. Speak, my beloved, and let no one dare to speak but you. Be quiet, my soul. Speak, love!

This is when you know all things without knowing anything. You do not presume that you possess all truth within yourself. On the contrary, you feel that you see nothing, that you can do nothing, and that you are nothing. You feel it and delight in it. But in this abandonment, you find everything you need, moment by moment, in the infinity of God. You find there the daily bread of knowledge, and everything else, without setting aside anything for the future. The anointing from above teaches you all truth while removing your own wisdom, pride, interests—and yes, even your will. It makes you content with your powerlessness, with a position below every creature. You are ready to yield to the worms of the earth and confess your most guarded miseries to the whole world, dreading unfaithfulness more than punishment or embarrassment.

Here is where the Spirit teaches you all truth because all truth is completely contained in this sacrifice of love, when the soul strips itself of everything and gives it all to God.

FIVE

Acceptance

The best rule you can follow is to accept everything that God sends you during the day, both outwardly and inwardly. Outwardly, disagreeable things must be accepted with courage, and pleasant things must not be allowed to seize your emotions. You resist the temptations of the former by accepting those things at once, and you resist the temptations of the latter by refusing to let those pleasant things into your heart.

The same course is necessary with the inward life. Whatever is bitter serves to crucify you, and it works out its benefit in your soul if you receive it simply, with a willingness that has no boundaries and a readiness that seeks no relief. Pleasant gifts, which are given to support your weakness by giving you an emotional comfort for your outward work, must be accepted in a different way. You must accept them because God sends them and not because they're pleasing. They must be used like any other medicine. You must accept them but not cling to them so that when God sees fit to withdraw them, you'll be neither depressed nor discouraged.

Presumption comes from attachment to these perceptible and passing gifts. You imagine that you have no concern for anything but the gifts of God, but you are really concerned with yourself, taking his mercy as your own and mistaking it for him. You then become discouraged when you discover that you've thus deceived yourself. However, the soul that is fed by God is not surprised at its own misery. It is instead delighted to find new proof that it can do nothing by itself, that God must do everything.

You must depend less upon perceptible joys and standards of wisdom that work out your own perfection and more upon simplicity, lowliness, renunciation of your own efforts, and perfect flexibility toward all the designs of grace. Everything else tends to celebrate your virtues, inspiring a secret reliance upon your own resources. Ask God to uproot everything in your heart that you have planted and to place there, with his own hands, the tree of life, which bears all kinds of fruits.

You must not be surprised if you frequently notice in yourself feelings of pride, of confidence in yourself, of desiring to follow your own inclinations in spite of what is right, of impatience with the weakness of others or of annoyance at your own condition. In those moments, let these feelings drop away like stones to the bottom of the sea. Gather yourself in God and wait until you're in the right frame of mind before acting. If the distraction of business or an active imagination hinders you from calmly and comfortably entering into such a state of mind, at least try to be quiet through the discipline of the will and the desire for unity with God. In that case, the will to be united works to deprive the soul of its own will, making it submissive in the hands of God.

If it happens that some emotion connected to base human nature should escape you, don't be discouraged. Continue onward. Quietly bear the shame of your sin before God without being held back by the pain of self-love at the betrayal of its weakness. Proceed confidently without being troubled by the anguish of a wounded pride that can't bear to see its own imperfection. Your sin will be useful in causing you to die to self and to become nothing before God. The true method of curing this defect is to become dead to the sensitivity of self-love without hindering the journey of grace that has been interrupted by this temporary unfaithfulness.

The main point is to renounce your own wisdom by walking simply, ready to give up the favor, respect, and approval of others whenever the path in which God leads you passes that way. You are not to meddle with things that God does not give you. You must follow God and never go before him. When he gives the signal, you must leave everything and follow him. If you hesitate, delay, lose courage, dilute what he wants you to do, indulge fears for your own comfort or safety, desire to shield yourself from suffering and disgrace, or try to find some excuse for not performing a difficult and painful duty, then you are truly guilty in his sight. God keep you from such unfaithfulness.

Nothing is more dreadful than this inward resistance to him. It is that sin against the Holy Spirit that the Lord says "will not be forgiven, either in this age or in the age to come." Other sins committed in the naiveté of good intentions will be useful if they produce humility and make you less important in your own eyes. But resisting the Spirit of God through pride and weak, worldly wisdom — careful about your own comfort in performing the work of God — is a sin that will gradually quench the Spirit of grace in your heart. God, jealous and rejected after so much mercy, will depart and leave you to your own resources. You will then travel around in a kind of circle instead of advancing with rapid strides along the king's highway. Your inward life will grow dim and dimmer, and you won't be able to discover the sure and deep-rooted source of your disease.

God wants to see in you a simplicity that will contain more of his wisdom and less of your own. He wants to see you lowly in your own eyes and as accepting as a baby. He wants to create in your heart that the childlike disposition that is so distasteful to the spirit of humans but so agreeable to the spirit of the gospel. Through this simplicity and lowliness, he will heal all the remnants of arrogant and self-confident wisdom in you. From the moment you give your trust to the Lord, you will say with David, "I am willing to look even more foolish than this, even to be humiliated in my own eyes!"

Six

Humility

Being humbled is a great mercy to a soul that receives it with steady faith. Nothing makes you so tender and forgiving toward the faults of others as a clear vision of your own faults. Even those faults that are most difficult to bear will be of service if you use them to produce humility.

To benefit from the humiliation of your faults, study them in all their deformity but do so without losing hope in God and without having any confidence in yourself. It does no good to be discouraged. Discouragement is merely the result of a disappointed and despairing self-love. You must bear with

43

yourself with neither flattery nor discouragement, a balance that is seldom attained. The true foundation of the spiritual building is utter despair in yourself, and this comes from a clear understanding of your own helplessness and unlimited confidence in God.

Do not imagine that you can do this by yourself. Everything within you is opposed to it. However, you can rejoice in the presence of God. Jesus has chosen to join you in all your weaknesses. He is a compassionate high priest who has voluntarily submitted to be tempted in all the ways that you are tempted. You must therefore find your strength in the one who became weak in order to strengthen you. Enrich yourself with his poverty, confidently shouting, "I can do all things through him who strengthens me!"

Imitate Jesus. Live as he lived, think as he thought, and be conformed to his image, which is the mark of righteousness. He was born in a stable. He had to flee to Egypt. He spent the first thirty years of his life in a workshop. He experienced hunger, thirst, and weariness. He was poor, despised, and miserable. He taught the truths of heaven, and no one listened. The powerful and the wise attacked him and arrested him. They tortured him frightfully. They treated him like a slave. They put him to death between two criminals, preferring to give freedom to a robber rather than let him escape. This was the life that the Lord chose to live, yet Christians today are horrified at any kind of humiliation, unable to bear even the slightest appearance of contempt.

To be a Christian is to imitate Jesus Christ. How can Christians expect to find Jesus if they don't look for him in the conditions of his earthly life — in loneliness and silence, in poverty and suffering, in persecution and contempt, in death and the cross? The saints find Jesus in heaven, in the brilliance of glory and indescribable pleasure, but that comes only after they have lived with him on earth in reproach, in pain, and in humility. How can you imitate Jesus if not in humility? Nothing else can bring you close to him. You can adore him as omnipotent, fear him as just, love him with all your heart as good and merciful, but you can only imitate him as humble, submissive, poor, and despised.

Compare your live with the life of Jesus Christ. He is the master, and you are the servant. He is all-powerful, and you are all weakness. He is lowered, and you are lifted up. Keep your frailty in mind so constantly that you will have nothing but contempt for yourself. You won't be able to look down on others and think about their faults when you see that you are filled with nothing else.

May you earnestly do this work. May you change the heart that is so rebellious into the heart of Jesus Christ. May your soul advance toward the holy soul of Jesus. May he enliven your soul and destroy all your aversions. Follow the path that the savior has marked for you because that is the only path that will lead you to him.

Those who are truly humble are surprised to hear praise for anything about themselves. They are gentle and peaceful, contrite and humble in their hearts, merciful and compassionate. They're quiet, cheerful, obedient, attentive, passionate in spirit, and incapable of strife. They always take the lowest place, rejoice when they are despised, and consider every one superior to themselves. They are forgiving of the faults of others because of their own. They are far from setting themselves ahead of anyone.

Lovely Jesus! You have suffered so many injuries and reproaches for my sake. Let me now honor and love them for your sake. Allow me to desire to share your life of humility. Let me follow in your footsteps, Jesus! I want to imitate you, but I cannot without the help of your grace. Humble and lowly savior, give me the understanding of a true Christian. In order that I can willingly despise myself, allow me to learn the lesson so incomprehensible to the human mind, that I must die to myself with an abandonment that will produce true humility.

SEVEN

Discouragement

Discouragement often arises from the fact that, in seeking God, you have not found him in a way that contents you. Your weak human nature, depressed and discouraged, becomes impatient with the restraints of the naked faith that strips away every outward support. It doesn't like to be traveling in the air, as it were, where it cannot watch its own progress towards perfection. Its pride is irritated by the sight of its imperfections, and it mistakes this feeling for humility. Out of self-love, it longs to see itself as perfect, and it's frustrated that it's not already so. It becomes impatient, arrogant, and angry with itself and everybody else.

Freedom from Self

What a sorry state, as if the work of God could be accomplished by such ill-humor, as if the peace of God could be attained through such inner restlessness. Martha, Martha! Why are you worried and anxious about so many things? Only one thing is necessary, to love him and sit attentively at his feet. When you are truly abandoned to God, all things are accomplished without the pursuit of useless labors. For the future, you desire whatever God desires, and you close your eyes to everything else. For the present, you yield yourself entire to fulfilling his plans. You allow yourself to be guided in perfect trust.

This daily doing of God's will is the arrival of his kingdom within you and, at the same time, your daily bread. Leave it all to him. Let him make it short or long, bitter or sweet. Let him do whatever he pleases with it. The best way to prepare for the future, whatever it may be, is to die to every desire of your own and yield yourself entirely to his will. In this frame of mind, you will be ready to receive all the grace you need for whatever God decides to develop within you and around you.

When you are made ready in this way for every moment, you begin to feel the rock under your feet at the very bottom of the abyss. You're as peaceful toward the past as toward the future. You're prepared to accept every imaginable evil about yourself, but you throw yourself blindly into the arms of God, forgetting and losing everything else. This forgetfulness of self is the perfect repentance. Becoming a Christian is nothing more than renouncing the self and accepting God — the sacrifice of self-love. It would be a thousand times more agreeable for you to accuse and condemn yourself, to torment you body and mind, rather than to simply forget yourself. Such self-abandonment is the annihilation of self-love, which no longer offers any nourishment. The heart begins to expand. You begin to feel lighter for having thrown aside the burden of the self that you used to carry.

51

The simplicity and straightness of the path is astonishing. You had thought you'd have to constantly struggle and strain on this path, but now you see that there isn't much to do. It's enough to look to God with confidence, without thinking about either the past or the future. You only have to look to him as a loving father who takes you by the hand and leads you through every moment. If one distraction or another happens to obscure him for a moment, you simply turn back to the one you have left without stopping to look any further at whatever distracted you. If you sin, you repent with a repentance that comes entirely from love. When you return to God, he makes you feel however you should feel. Sin seems hideous to you, but you love the humility that it causes, which is why God allowed it.

Just as your pride's contemplation of your weaknesses are bitter, disheartening, and frustrating, so the turning of the soul towards God is composed, peaceful, and sustained by confidence. You will find through experience how this simple, peaceful turning toward God helps you much more than all your frustration and anger at the weaknesses within you. The moment you perceive that you have done something wrong, you only need to turn quietly to God in faith. Don't stop to argue with yourself. That offers you nothing. When you attack yourself for your wretchedness, you are only consulting with yourself. Poor wisdom will come from wherever God is absent.

Whose hand can pull you out of the muck? Your own? Alas, you are buried deeper than thought, and you cannot help yourself—in fact, this muck is nothing *but* self. Your entire problem is that you're unable to leave yourself. Do you really think, then, that you improve your chances by constantly dwelling upon your weaknesses and feeding your sensitivity by focusing on your foolishness? You will only make the problem worse. However, even the gentlest look toward God will calm your heart.

His presence is what causes to leave self behind, and when he has done that, you are a peace. How do you move forward then? Simply by turning gently towards God. By faithfully persisting in that, you will gradually make a habit of turning toward him whenever you see that you have wandered from him.

As for the natural discouragement that comes from depression, that is a physical matter for a doctor to address. While it is true that this reoccurs regularly, it shouldn't be something that you choose. Whenever God allows it to occur, you should bear it in peace, just as you accept from his hands fevers or other physical ailments. The state of your emotions is not the issue. What matters is the state of your will. Desire to have whatever you have and not to have whatever you lack. You should not even desire to be rescued from your suffering, for it's God's place to assign both your suffering and your joy. In the midst of affliction, you must rejoice as the apostle did, but this is not the joy of emotions but of the will.

Unbelievers are miserable in the midst of their pleasures because they're never content with their condition. They always desire to remove some thorn or to add some flower. The believing soul, on the other hand, has a will that is perfectly free. Without questioning, it accepts whatever bitter blessings God brings. It wills them, loves them, and embraces them. It wouldn't choose to be free from them, even if a simple wish could free them, for such a wish would be an action that arises from the self, that runs contrary to abandonment to providence, and the believing soul wants that abandonment to always be complete.

If anything can bring a soul into an abundant place, it is this absolute abandonment to God. It infuses the soul with a peace that flow "like a river, and a righteousness like the waves of the sea." If anything can calm the soul, dissolve its worries, dispel its fears, sweeten its sufferings with the anointing of love, give strength to it for all its work, and spread the joy of the Holy Spirit in its words and expression, it is this simple, free, childlike rest in the arms of God.

EIGHT

Suffering

It is hard to accept the goodness of God when he burdens those he loves with suffering. "Why," you ask, "should God take pleasure in making us suffer? Couldn't he make us good without also making us miserable?" Yes, he undoubtedly could, for all things are possible with God. He holds in his all-powerful hands the hearts of all people, and he directs them as he chooses, just as a skilled worker can direct a stream flowing down a hill. However, even though God is able to save his children from suffering, he has chosen not to, just as he has chosen not to create people as fully grown adults but to allow them to grow up by degrees amid all the dangers and frailties of infancy and childhood. In the matter of suffering, he is the master. You can only adore in silence the depths of his wisdom — without comprehending it.

Even so, you can see clearly that you could never become wholly good without becoming humble, unselfish, and inclined to direct everything to God without any anxious, self-centered actions. The work of grace to detach you from the self and destroy your self-love could not be anything other than painful without a miracle, and neither in his works of grace nor works of providence does God give miracles lightly.

To see a person who is full of self become instantly dead to all self-interest and self-awareness would be as great a marvel as for a sleeping infant to wake up one morning as a full-grown adult. In works of grace as well as of nature, God works in mysterious ways, concealing his work beneath an imperceptible sequence of events. He accomplishes his plans gradually, and he does so through methods that appear to be the most simple and effective so that human wisdom can attribute the success to the methods. Otherwise, every act of God would appear to be a miracle, and the state of faith, in which God wants his children to live, would come to an end.

This state of faith is necessary for the development of those who are good by forcing them to sacrifice their reason in a life so full of darkness. It also blinds those who, because of their presumption, deserve judgment. They see the works of God but don't understand them. They see nothing in those works except for the effects of physical laws. They are barren of true understanding because true understanding is only available to those who distrust their own abilities. Proud human wisdom is not worthy of God's instruction.

God makes the working of grace slow and obscure, then, so that he can keep you in the darkness of faith. He uses the inconsistency and ingratitude of others, along with the disappointment and overindulgence that comes with prosperity, to detach you from them both. He frees you from self by showing you your weaknesses and perversions. All of these works seem perfectly natural, and it is through this succession of natural methods that he purifies you as if over a slow fire. You would like to be consumed at once by the flames of pure love, but that would scarcely cost you anything. Only excessive self-love desires to become perfect in a moment and at so cheap a price.

Why do you rebel against the length of the journey? It's because you're wrapped up in self. God must destroy this infatuation that is a constant hindrance to his work. He thus prepares a series of events that will gradually detach you from others and separate you from self. The work is painful, but it's necessary because of this rottenness, and the same rottenness is what makes the work so distressing. If you then suffer greatly, it's because the evil is great.

When bodies are sound, surgeons have no need for the knife. They only cut to the depth of the wound and the diseased parts of the body. Are surgeons cruel because they cut to the bone? On the contrary, they cut to the bone with both skill and love. They would treat their own beloved children in the same way. It is the same with God. He never afflicts you — if you want to put it in those terms — except against his own, loving inclination. His fatherly heart is not gratified by the sight of your misery. He cuts to the bone so that he can heal the disease in your soul. He must snatch away whatever you hold too fondly, along with all that you love against his will and his rights.

In this, he does just as people do with children. The children cry because their parents take away the knife, which is their amusement but which might also be their death. In the same way, you weep, you become discouraged, you cry out and are ready to murmur against God like children angry with their parents. God lets you weep, and he secures your salvation. He afflicts you only to mend you. Even when he seems to overwhelm you, he intends nothing but good. He intends only to spare you the evil that you were preparing for yourself. The things you lament for a little while now would have caused you to mourn forever. God only deprives you of the things that you cherish in order to teach you how to love them purely, solidly, and moderately and to secure for you their eternal enjoyment in his own arms. He does you a thousand times more good than you could ask—or even imagine—on your own.

All that people treasure means nothing in the eyes of God. A little more or less of life is a difference that disappears in the light of his eternity. What does it matter if this fragile vessel, this clay temple, is broken and reduced to ashes a little sooner or later? People are thrown into consternation at the death of others in the prime of life. "What a terrible loss!" the world cries out. But who has lost anything? The dead? They have lost a few years of vanity, illusion, and threats to their immortal souls. God has snatched them from the midst of their sins, separating them from a corrupt world and their own weakness.

What difference is there between two people who lived a century ago? One died twenty years before the other, but now both are gone. The separation that then seemed so abrupt and so long seems like nothing now—and was, in fact, short. The things that are separated by death will soon be reunited, and no trace of separation will be visible. People look upon themselves as immortal, or at least as living for ages. Folly and madness! Life flows past like a rushing stream. All that is gone is like a dream, and even while you contemplate all that exists today, it vanishes into the abyss of the past.

The disgust at suffering comes from the frailty of self-love. The sick man thinks the night will never end because he can't sleep, but this night is no longer than others. The sufferings are great, but timidity enlarges them. The way to lessen the suffering is to abandon yourself courageously into the hands of God. You must suffer, but the result of your pain is to purify your soul and make you worthy of him.

Sometimes you suffer without really knowing that you suffer. At other times, you suffer and know that you bear it poorly, but you carry this second and heavier cross without impatience. True love always continues moving forward, not by its own strength but by regarding itself as nothing. Then you are truly happy. The cross is no longer a cross when there is no self to suffer beneath it and bear its good and evil.

Only true and pure love delights to endure suffering, for nothing else is perfectly abandoned. In pure love, unselfish and abandoned, the soul is silently nourished by the cross and union with the crucified savior—without any thoughts about the severity of its sufferings. There exists only a single, simple desire that allows God to see the soul just as it is. It says nothing and does nothing. It has nothing else to do but suffer.

NINE

Faith

Those who are united to God only to the extent that they enjoy pleasure and comfort are like those who followed the Lord, not to hear his teaching but because they ate the bread and were filled. With Peter, they say, "Rabbi, it is good that we are here. Let us put up three shelters," but they don't know what they're saying. After being intoxicated with the joys of the mountain, they deny the Son of God and refuse to follow him to Calvary.

Not only do they desire pleasures, they also seek illuminations. Their minds are curious to understand, and their hearts want to be filled with gentle and flattering emotions. They desire extraordinary revelations that can be regarded as supernatural gifts, a mark of special favor from God. It may be a refined ambition because it's entirely spiritual, but it's still merely ambition, a desire to experience, enjoy, and possess God and his gifts. Is this dying to self? Is this the way in which the righteous will live by faith?

The apostle presents "a still more excellent way." It's the way of love, which "doesn't insist on her own way" and—to adopt the apostle's language—doesn't seek to be adorned but allows herself to be unclothed. The soul doesn't seek pleasure so much as God himself, whose will she longs to fulfill. If she finds pleasure in devotion, she doesn't rest in that pleasure but uses it to strengthen her weakness, just as the injured use a cane to help them walk but will set the cane aside when they're fully recovered. In the same way, the gentle and childlike soul that God fed with milk in the beginning allows herself to be weaned when God sees that it's time to nourish the soul with solid food.

You must not remain an infant, forever clinging to the breast of heavenly comforts. With Paul, you must "give up childish ways." Your early joys were perfect for drawing you forward, for detaching you from worldly pleasures by offering pleasure of a purer kind, and for leading you into a life of prayer and reflection. However, remaining in a continual state of enjoyment removes the experience of the cross. Living in the enthusiasm of devotion that keeps paradise open before you is not dying on the cross and becoming nothing.

This life of illumination and perceptible pleasure is a dangerous trap if you become so attached to it that you desire nothing else. Those who have no other attraction to prayer will soon quit both prayer and God as soon as this source of satisfaction dries up. Saint Theresa says that a vast number of souls stop praying at the very moment when their devotion is just beginning to be real. How many there are who, having been raised too gently in Jesus Christ and having too much fondness for the milk of his word, turn away and abandon the inner life as soon as God begins to wean them. They mistake the porch of the temple for the inner sanctuary. They seek the death of their base, outward desires so that they can lead a delicious life of inward self-satisfaction.

From this comes much unfaithfulness and disappointment, even among those who seem to be the most fervent and devoted. Those who talk the loudest about abandonment, death to self, the darkness of faith, and desolation are often the most surprised and discouraged when their comforts are removed. As long as the pleasure lasts, they think that they will never desert God. In their prosperity, they say, "I will never be shaken." However, the moment the intoxication ends, they give it up all for lost, thus substituting their own pleasure and imagination for God.

How excellent instead is the path pointed out by John of the Cross, who desires you to believe without seeing and love without desiring to feel love. Only that kind of naked faith is a reliable guard against delusion. You're on a path that isn't subject to delusion when your life is no longer founded upon imagination, feeling, pleasure, or extraordinary illumination. You receive the comfort God sends in the simplicity of the gospel but not abiding in it, not judging, always obeying, believing that it is easy to be deceived and that others can set you straight, living every moment with simplicity and honorable intention, and following the light of faith in the present moment. Experience will demonstrate better than anything else how much more reliable this path is than the path of illuminations and perceptible pleasures.

The path of naked faith is the deepest and most complete death of self. Inward pleasures and revelations compensate self-love for all of its outward sacrifices, but allowing yourself to be stripped outwardly by providence and inwardly by the night of pure faith is a complete sacrifice. It produces a condition that is the farthest possible

69

from self-deception. Those who try to protect themselves from deception with a continual stream of emotions and assurances are assuredly exposing themselves — by that strategy — to deception. Those who follow the direction of the love that strips them and the faith that walks in darkness, without seeking any other support, avoid all the sources of error and delusion.

The author of the *Imitation of Christ* writes that if God takes away your inward pleasures, it should be your pleasure to remain pleasureless. How beloved of God is a soul thus crucified, a soul that rests peacefully on the cross, seeking only to die with Jesus. You haven't lost God when you're deprived of feeling him. That is merely impatience in the time of trial, the restlessness of a pampered and delicate nature, a weariness of abandonment, and a secret return to self after having been set apart to God. Where are those will not stop on the road to death? If they persevere to the end, they will receive a crown of life.

Ten

Prayer

Many are tempted to believe that they no longer pray when they cease to enjoy any clear pleasure from the act of prayer. However, if they will remember that perfect prayer is simply another name for loving God, they will be set right.

Prayer does not consist of enjoyable feelings, nor the enchantment of a roused imagination, nor that illumination of the intellect that easily reveals the deepest truths in God, nor even in the sure comfort of seeing God. All these things are outwards gifts from his hand. In their absence, love can exist even more purely because the soul can then attach itself immediately and only to God instead of to his gifts. This is the love of naked faith that is the death of human nature. It leaves human nature nothing to stand on. When you're convinced that all is lost, that same conviction is your evidence that all is gained.

Pure love is only in the will. It's not emotional love because the imagination has no part in it. It loves without feeling in the same way that faith believes without seeing. You don't need to fear that this love is an imaginary thing. Nothing can be less imaginary than the will that is separate from all imagination. The more that the workings of the mind are purely intellectual and spiritual, the nearer they are not only to reality but to the holiness that God requires. Faith is fully active while humility is preserved. Such love is pure because it's the love of God in and for God. You are attached to him but not because of the pleasure that he gives you. You follow him but not because of the loaves and fishes.

"What?" some may say. "Is it possible that a simple will united with God is the whole of piety? How can we be sure that this decision is not a mere idea, a trick of the imagination, instead of a true willing of the soul?"

I would indeed believe that it was a deception if it wasn't also the parent of faithfulness in all fitting situations. A good tree bears good fruit, and a true will makes you truly earnest and diligent in doing the will of God. In this life, however, a true will is still compatible with little failures, which God allows so that the soul will be humbled. If you only experience these small, daily weaknesses, then you should not be discouraged. You should instead draw from them their proper fruit — humility.

True virtue and pure love reside only in the will. Isn't it a great challenge to always desire the Supreme Good whenever he is seen, to keep the mind steadily turned towards him and to bring it back to him when you find that it has wandered, to desire nothing except for what he commands? In the absence of all perceivable joy, isn't it a challenge to remain steady in a spirit of submissive, irreclaimable sacrifice?

73

Freedom from Self

Do you think it is nothing to repress all the uneasy thoughts of self-love, to continually press ahead without knowing where you go, to stop thinking self-satisfied thoughts of self—or at the least, to think of yourself as you would of others? Do you think it is nothing to follow the indications of providence within one moment and no further? Isn't this more likely to cause the death of the old Adam than elevated ideas are? With those ideas, you are in fact thinking only of the self or outward actions, and in doing those ideas, you congratulate the self for its accomplishment.

The desire to continually be assured that you are doing well is a kind of infidelity to simple faith. In fact, it is God's will that you should ignore the desire to know what you are doing. You will never understand it, and you are dawdling along the way when you try to figure out the way. The safest and shortest path is to renounce, forget, and abandon the self. Through faithfulness to God, you should think no more

74

about it. This is the whole of religion — to move out of the self and self-love in order to move into God.

As to involuntary wandering thoughts, they do not hinder love because love is in the will, and the will only wanders when it chooses to wander. As soon as you notice that you have wandered, instantly leave your wandering and return to God. Thus, while the outward senses of the bride are asleep, the heart watches. Its love has no interruption. Loving parents do not always have their children distinctly in mind. They think and imagine a thousand things that have nothing to do with their children. But those thoughts don't interfere with parental affection. The moment that their thoughts rest again upon their children, they love. In the depths of their soul, they feel that although they have not been thinking about their children, they have not for an instant ceased to love them. This is how your love should be to your heavenly Father — simple, trusting, confident, and free from anxiety.

If your imagination flies away and your thoughts wander, you shouldn't worry. These things are not "the hidden person of the heart with the imperishable beauty of a gentle and quiet spirit" that Peter speaks about. Whenever you can, you should merely turn your thoughts back toward the face of the beloved without being bothered by your wanderings. When he sees fit to enable you to maintain a more constant sense of his presence, he will do so.

He sometimes removes that sense of his presence for the sake of your advancement. It occupies your attention with too many reflections that are true distractions, diverting your mind from a simple and direct look toward God and drawing you away from the protection of pure faith. In these reflections, you often look for a resting place for your self-love. You try to extract evidence from them that will offer comfort to the self. Thus the warmth of your feelings can cause you to wander. On the other hand, you never pray so purely as when you are tempted to believe that you do not pray at all. You fear that you pray poorly, but you should only fear being abandoned to the desolation of sinful human nature, to philosophical infidelity, to a perpetual search for evidence of the will working in faith, to impatient desires for outward and emotional encouragement.

There is no more bitter penance than this condition of pure faith without any perceptible support. To me, that seems to be the most effective, the most crucifying, and the least deceptive. Strange temptation! Christians impatiently search for perceivable encouragement because they fear they're not penitent enough. Shouldn't they instead consider the renunciation of that encouragement that they are so powerfully tempted to seek as proof of their penitence? Remember the Lord, abandoned by his father on the cross. All perceptions and thoughts of God were withdrawn so that God would be hidden from him. This was truly the final blow to fall upon the man of sorrows, the consummation of his sacrifice.

You will never abandon yourself to God as much as when he seems to abandon you. You should enjoy enlightenment and encouragement when it's his pleasure to give it to you, but you should attach yourself to him, not to his gifts. When he plunges you into the night of pure faith, you must still press on through that agonizing darkness.

Moments are worth days during this trial. The soul is troubled yet at peace. Not only is God hidden from the soul, but the soul is hidden from itself so that everything will be done in faith. The soul is discouraged, but it still experiences an immovable will to bear everything that God chooses to inflict. It wills all and accepts all, even the troubles that test its faith. Thus, at the very height of the storm, the waters beneath are secretly calm and at peace, because the soul's will is one with God's will. Praise to the Lord who does such great things in his children in spite of their unworthiness.

Eleven

The Presence of God

The true source of union with God is contained in God's command to Abraham: "Walk before me and be blameless." The presence of God calms the soul and gives it peace and rest even during the day and in the midst of its work. However, you must give yourself to God without holding anything back, for once you have found God, you have nothing to seek from the world. You must sacrifice even the dearest of your friendships. The dearest friends have entered into your heart, and the jealous bridegroom requires the whole of your heart for himself.

It takes no great amount of time to love God, to be refreshed by his presence, to lift your heart to him, to worship him in the depths of your soul, or to offer to him all you do and all you suffer. This is the true kingdom of God within you, a kingdom that cannot be disturbed. When the distraction of the senses and the liveliness of the imagination hold the soul back from that sweet and peaceful state of union with God, you should at least be at peace in terms of your desires. In that case, the desire to be in God's presence is a sufficient state of devotion for the time being.

From time to time, try to awaken within yourself the desire of being set apart to God to the extent of all your powers. In your intellect, desire to know him and think about him. In your will, desire to love him. Desire, too, that your physical senses may be set apart for him in all their workings. Be careful, then, how you voluntarily engage in things — externally or internally — that distract the intellect and the will, drawing them out of themselves so that they find it difficult to return to the presence of God.

The moment you discover that anything causes excessive pleasure or joy within you, you should separate your heart from it. To prevent the heart from seeking its rest in a part of creation, you should present that thing to God, the true object of love, the sovereign good. If you are faithful in breaking off all attachments to created things — that is, if you prevent them from entering those depths of the soul that the Lord reserves for himself, from abiding there as respected, adored, and beloved things — you will soon experience that pure joy which God never fails to give to a soul that is freed and detached from all human affections.

Whenever you perceive within yourself anxious desires for anything, whatever they may be, and find that your nature is rushing to do what needs to be done — to say something, see something, or do something — you should stop and calm the rashness of your thoughts and the disturbance of your actions, for God has said that his Spirit does not abide in anxiety.

Be careful not to pay too much attention to what is going on around you, either. It is an abundant source of distraction. As soon as you find what God requires in any new situation, stop there and separate yourself from everything else. In this way, you will always keep the depths of the soul free and serene, ridding yourself of many things that disturb the hearts and prevent it from turning easily toward God.

An excellent way to preserve inner solitude and freedom of soul is to make it a rule, at the conclusion of every action, to put an end to all thoughts about it, along with all reflective acts of self-love, whether from vain joy or sorrow. Happy are those whose minds contain only what is needed, who do not think of it except when it is time to think of it. God, then, is the one who stirs their thoughts, calling them to do his will as soon as it is revealed, rather than their own minds laboriously looking ahead and searching for his will.

In short, you should be in the habit of returning to the presence of God during the day and in the midst of your work by simply looking toward God. In this way, you will silence all the activity of the heart when the hearts seem to be even slightly agitated. Separate yourself from everything that doesn't come from God, holding back all unnecessary thoughts and musings. Utter no unnecessary words. Only seek God within yourself, and you will find him without fail, and with him, you will find joy and peace.

While you're outwardly busy, be more occupied with God than with everything else. To be working correctly, you must be in his presence and working for him. At the sight of the majesty of God, your inner life should become calm and remain tranquil. A single word of the savior once calmed a furious, stormy sea. One look of his to you, and of yours to him, should always perform the same miracle within you.

Lift your heart to God often. He will purify, enlighten, and guide it. This was the daily practice of the holy psalmist: "I keep my eyes always on the Lord." May you often use the beautiful

words of the same holy prophet: "Whom have I
in heaven but you? And there is nothing on earth
that I desire besides you." Don't wait for a leisure
hour when you can lock your doors. The time
you use to regret that you have no time to seek
the presence of God could be profitably used to
seek the presence of God. Turn your heart toward
God in a simple, intimate spirit, full of confidence in him. The most interrupted moments,
even while eating or listening to others, are still
valuable. The tiresome and idle talk of others,
instead of annoying you, will afford the delight
of using that time to seek God. Thus all things
work together for good for those who love God.

Read according to your needs and desires,
but with frequent stops in order to seek the presence of God. A word or two, simple and full of
the Spirit of God, will be like hidden manna to
you. You may forget the words, but the effect
remains. The words of the Spirit work in secret,
feeding and enriching the soul.

Twelve

The Will of God

The heart of virtue is the orientation of the will. This is what the Lord wishes to teach you when he says, "The kingdom of God is within you." It's not a question of broad knowledge, of impressive talents, nor even of great work. It's a simple matter of having a heart and loving.

Outward works are the fruits and consequences of loving. The spring of all good things flows upward from the bottom of the soul. Some virtues are appropriate to certain situations and not to others. Some are good at one time, and some at another. However, an upright will is profitable at all times and in all situations. The kingdom of God within you consists in your willing whatever God wills — at all times, in all things, and without holding back. This is how his kingdom comes because his will is then done on earth as it is in heaven. You choose nothing except for what his sovereign will determines.

Blessed are the poor in spirit. Blessed are they who are stripped of everything — even of their own wills — so that they no longer belong to themselves. How poor in spirit they become when they have given all things to God. But how is it that your will becomes righteous when it conforms unreservedly to the will of God? You choose whatever he chooses. Whatever he does not choose, you do not choose. You attach your feeble will to that all-powerful will that rules over everything. In this way, nothing will ever happen that is contrary to your wishes because nothing can ever happen that is contrary to the will of God. You thus find an inexhaustible source of peace and comfort in his good intentions.

The interior life is the beginning of the blessed peace of the saints, who continually cry out, "Amen! Amen!" They adore God, they praise God, and they honor God in everything. They see him constantly before themselves, and in all things, his fatherly hand is the sole focus of their contemplation. There are no longer any evils because even the most terrible things that happen work together for good, as Paul says, for those who love God. Can they call their suffering evil if God ordains it in order to purify them and make them worthy of himself?

Put all your worries, then, into the hands of so good a father and allow him to do as he pleases. Be content to adopt his will in all things and abandon your own will entirely. How can you keep back anything of your own when you don't even belong to yourself? The slave owns nothing. How much less, then, should you own anything when you yourself are nothingness and sin, owing everything to pure grace? God has only given you a will, free and capable of self-possession, so that you can more generously repay the gift by returning it to its rightful owner.

You own nothing but your will. All the rest belongs elsewhere. Disease removes life and health. Riches make wings for themselves and fly away. Intellectual talents depend upon the condition of the body. Because the only thing that really belongs to you is your will, God is particularly jealous for it. He gave a will to everyone, not so that anyone should hold it back, but so that everyone might return it to him without the slightest reservation. If the smallest desire of your own remains, the smallest hesitation, you steal from God, opposing the order he has created, for all things come from him, and to him, all things are due.

So many souls are so full of self. They want to do good and serve God — but in a way that pleases themselves. They want to impose rules upon God about how he draws them to himself. They want to serve him and possess him, but they aren't willing to abandon themselves to him and be possessed by him. What a resistance they have for him, even when they appear to be full of zeal and enthusiasm. In one sense, their spiritual abundance clearly becomes an obstacle to their progress because they keep everything as their own, even their virtues, constantly gathering for their own sake, even in good works. These passionate and illuminated souls, always walking virtuously on a path of their own choosing, are inferior to the humble hearts that renounce their own lives and every selfish motive, rejecting all desires except for those that God gives, moment by moment, in conformity to his gospel and providence.

This is what the Lord means when he says, "Whoever wants to be my disciple must deny themselves and take up their cross and follow me." You must follow Jesus Christ, step by step, and not create a path for yourself. You can only follow him by denying yourself, and this means abandoning every right you hold to yourself without holding anything back. As Paul says, "You are not your own." Not a single thing remains that belongs to you.

Desiring to serve God in one place rather than another or in this way rather than in that — isn't that desiring to serve him in your own way rather than in his? Truly denying yourself is to be equally ready for all things, to desire everything and nothing, to leave yourself in his hands like a toy in the hands of a child, to set no boundaries to your abandonment because the perfect reign of God cannot abide them. This is what it means to treat God like a god and yourself like a creature made solely for his use.

There is no peace for those who resist God. If there is joy in the world, it is reserved for a pure conscience, and for those who do not have that, the whole earth is full of troubles and anguish. The peace of God is so different from the peace of the world. It calms the passions, preserves the purity of the conscience, unites people to God, and strengthens them against temptations. It is inseparable from righteousness. The peace of the soul consists of absolute submission to the will of God: "Martha,

Martha, you are anxious and troubled about many things, but only one thing is necessary." The pain people suffer from so many events comes from the fact that they aren't entirely abandoned to God in everything that happens. So put all things into his hands, and offer them to him in your heart as a sacrifice beforehand.

The moment you stop desiring anything according to your own mind and begin to desire everything just as God desires it, you will be free from your former tormenting thoughts and anxieties about your own concerns. You will no longer have anything to conceal or take care of. Until then, you will be troubled. You will be divided in your thoughts and pleasures, easily dissatisfied with others and rarely satisfied with yourself. You will be full of reservations and distrust. Until your good intentions become truly humble and simple, they will merely torment you. Your religious discipline, however sincere, will be the source of internal reproach more than of support or consolation. However, if you will abandon your whole heart to God, you will be full of peace and joy in the Holy Spirit.

Alas for you, if you continue to have regard for humans while doing the work of God. In choosing what will guide you, humans must be counted as nothing. The slightest regard for their opinion dries up the stream of grace. It increases your indecision. You yourself will suffer, and besides that, you will displease God.

How can you refuse to give all your love to God, who first loved you with the tender love of a father? He pitied your weakness, understanding clearly the mire from which he has rescued you. When a soul is filled with this love, it enjoys a peace of conscience. It becomes content and happy. It requires neither greatness nor reputation nor pleasure nor any of the dying gifts of this age. It only desires the will of God, always waiting with joyful expectation for the bridegroom.

THIRTEEN

Virtue

Christian virtue is not that rigorous, tedious, cramped thing that many imagine. It demands an entire surrender of everything to God from the depths of the soul, and the moment this takes place, whatever you do for him becomes easy. Those who belong to God without holding back are content in every condition because they only desire what he desires, to do for him whatever he wants them to do. They strip themselves of everything, and in this nakedness, they find all things restored a hundred times over. They have a peaceful conscience, a free spirit, the sweet abandonment of themselves and their possessions into the hand of God, the joy of seeing the light always increasing in their hearts, and finally the freedom of their souls from slavery to the fears and desires of this world. These things constitute that return of happiness that the true children of God receive a hundredfold in the midst of their suffering when they remain faithful.

It's true that they are sacrificed, but they are sacrificed to the one they love best. They suffer, but they prefer that anguish to all the false joys of the world. Their bodies are subject to excruciating pain. Their imaginations are troubled. Their minds become listless and weak. However, their wills are firm and peacefully quiet within their souls, and they respond with a joyful "Amen!" to every blow from the hand that desires to perfect the sacrifice of their souls.

What God requires is a will no longer divided between him and others—a simple, pliable will that desires what he desires, that rejects nothing but what he rejects, that chooses without reservation whatever he chooses, and that under no pretext desires what he does not desire. In this state of mind, all things are right. Even amusements become acceptable in his sight.

Blessed are they who thus give themselves to God. They are rescued from their passions, from the opinions of others, from their malice, from the tyranny of their teachings, from their cold and miserable ridicule, from the misfortunes that the world blames on chance, from the infidelity and fickleness of friends, from the lies and traps of enemies, from the wretchedness and shortness of life, from the horrors of an ungodly death, from the cruel remorse that follows sinful pleasures, and finally from the everlasting condemnation of God. True Christians are rescued from this multitude of evil because by putting their will into the hands of God, they only desire what he desires and thus find comfort in the midst of all their suffering by faith and the hope that comes with it.

What weakness it is, then, to worry about devoting ourselves entirely to God and moving too deeply into such a desirable a state. Happy are those who throw themselves headlong, as it were, with their eyes shut, into the arms of "the father of mercies and God of all comfort." Their only desire then is to know the will of God for them. They fear nothing so much as not seeing all of his requirements. As soon as they see a new understanding of his law, they're overwhelmed with joy, like a miser who finds a treasure.

No matter what suffering might overcome the true children of God, they accept and desire everything that happens. They don't want anything that the father chooses to remove. The more they love God, the more they're filled with contentment. The most severe virtue, far from being a burden, only makes their yoke lighter. What foolishness, then, to worry about being too devoted to God—to fear happiness, to fear the love of God in all things, to fear having too much courage in inevitable suffering, too much comfort in the love of God, and too much detachment from the passions that make them miserable.

You must refuse, then, to place your affections on the things of the earth so that you can instead place them exclusively on God. I do not say that you must abandon them entirely. If your life is already moral and ordered, you only have to change the secret motive of your actions into love, and then you can continue almost the same way of life. God does not overthrow your place in the world or the duties that come with them, but you can now serve God by doing the same work that you used to do to please the world and yourself.

The difference is that instead of being driven by pride, by overwhelming passion, and by the malicious judgment of the world, you will act with freedom, with courage, and with hope in God. You'll be enlivened with confidence. The hope of eternal things, which draw near as the things of the world draw back, will support you in the midst of suffering. The love of God will give you wings to fly in his ways, raising you above all your misery. Is this hard to believe? Experience will convince you. As the psalmist says, "Oh, taste and see that the Lord is good!"

The Son of God says to every Christian, without exception, "Whoever wants to be my disciple must deny themselves and take up their cross and follow me." The broad path leads to destruction. You must walk on the narrow path even if only a few travel on it. Only the violent take the kingdom by force. You must be born again, renounce and hate yourself, become a child, be poor in spirit, and mourn so that you may be comforted. You must not be a part of this world, which is cursed because of its sins.

Many are fearful about these truths, and their fear arises from this—while they know the demanding nature of religion, they don't know its gifts or the spirit of love that makes everything easy. They're not aware that religion leads to the highest virtue while providing peace through a principle of love that smooths every rough place. Those who in truth and deed are entirely set apart for God are always happy. They prove that the yoke of the redeemer is easy and that his burden light, that the peace of the soul is found in him, and that just as he promises, he gives rest to those who are weary and burdened.

But how unhappy are those poor, weak souls who are divided between God and the world. They desire, and they do not desire. They're torn apart by their passions and their remorse. They fear the judgment of God and the opinions of others. They dislike evil, but they're ashamed of the good. They suffer the pains of virtue without enjoying its comforts. If they could only have a little courage—just enough to despise the vain talk, the cold sneers, and the rash judgments of humans—what peace they would enjoy in the arms of God.

Desiring to remain in your present situation is dangerous to your salvation, unworthy of God and of yourself, and destructive to your peace of mind. Your whole life has only been given to you so that you can advance with rapid strides towards the heavenly country. The world draws back like a deceptive shadow, and eternity already approaches to receive you. Why do you linger and look back while up ahead, the light of the father of mercies is shining on you? Hurry to reach the kingdom of God!

All the idle pretexts that you use to hide your reservations toward God are instantly scattered by the first commandment of the law: "Love the Lord your God with all your heart and with all your soul and with all your strength and with all your mind." Notice how the Holy Spirit brings together many expressions in this passage in order to block all the reservations that the soul might unfairly have against this jealous love. You must love God not only with the whole extent and strength of the soul but with all the intensity of the intellect. How then can you decide that you love him if you cannot make up your mind to accept his law and immediately give yourself to the fulfillment of his blessed will?

Those who fear that they will discover too clearly what this love demands are indeed far from having the active and unceasing affection that this commandment requires. There is only one way to love God, and that is to take no step except with him and for him—to do, with generous self-abandonment, everything that he requires.

Those who live a life of partial virtue but who also want to enjoy a little of the world think that this is a small thing. However, they run the risk of being included among those lukewarm ones that God will spit out of his mouth. God is not pleased with souls that say, "I will go this far and no farther." Should the creature make laws for the creator? What would a master say about servants or a king about subjects who are willing to serve but only as they wish, who fear that they will become too invested in his service or his interests, who are ashamed to openly acknowledge that they serve him? What will the king of kings say to you if you serve him in this way?

The time for departure is never far off. It is near, close at hand. Be ready for it. You've seen that those who are today highly honored and respected by others are tomorrow surprised by death and laid side by side in the tomb. The world is nothing but misery, vanity, and foolish-ness—a phantom. At any moment you might leave this poor place, this object of so much insane attachment. So despise this miserable world that is falling to pieces on every side. Love that eternal beauty that never grows old and that preserves in endless youth those who love nothing else.

FOURTEEN

Vigilance

Wise and careful travelers watch every step, keeping their eyes on that part of the road that is immediately in front of them. The soul that God truly leads by the hand — I am not speaking now about those who are learning to walk or who are still looking for the road — should pay attention to its path, but it should do so with a simple, tranquil vigilance that is confined to the present moment and without restlessness from a love of self. Its attention should be continually focused on the will of God in order to fulfill his will every moment. It shouldn't be engaged in reflections designed to assure itself of its condition when God prefers it to be uncertain.

The psalmist says, "My eyes are ever toward the Lord, for he will pluck my feet out of the net." Notice how the psalmist safely watches over his feet on a path filled with traps. Instead of keeping his eyes focused on the ground to scrutinize every step, he raises them to the Lord. You will never watch over yourself more carefully than when you walk in the presence of God, as God commanded Abraham. And, in fact, what should be the goal of all your vigilance? To follow the will of God step by step.

If you never lose sight of the presence of God, then you never cease to watch over yourself, and always with a simple, lovely, quiet, and disinterested vigilance. On the other hand, vigilance that comes from a desire for reassurance is harsh, restless, and full of self. You must walk not in your own light but in the light of God. You can't behold the holiness of God without feeling horror at the smallest of your sins.

In addition to the presence of God and a state of mindfulness, you can add the examination of conscience, as the moment requires. This examination, however, should be done in a way that grows more and more simple, relaxed, and free from restless self-contemplation. You must not examine yourself for your own satisfaction but to conform to the advice you receive and to do the will of God.

Small sins become great and even monstrous in your eyes as the pure light of God increases within you, just as the rising sun reveals the true shape of objects that were dimly and confusedly perceived during the night. As the inward light increases, you can be sure that the imperfections you've seen will be seen as much greater and more deadly in nature than you imagine they are now. In addition, you will see the crowd of other sins about whose existence you haven't had even the slightest suspicion. In that light, you will find the weaknesses necessary to strip away all confidence in your own strength, but far from discouraging you, this understanding will work to destroy your self-reliance, to tear to the ground the house of pride. Nothing so clearly marks the solid progress of a soul as this ability to see its own depravity without being troubled or discouraged.

It is an important rule to hold back from doing something wrong whenever you see it in time, and when you do not hold back, you must bear the humiliation of the sin with courage. If you perceive a sin before it is committed, you must make sure that you do not resist and stifle the Spirit of God that inwardly warns you about it. The Spirit is easily offended and very jealous. He desires to be listened to and obeyed. He withdraws if he's displeased. Even the slightest resistance to him is a sin because everything must yield to him the instant he is perceived. Sins of haste and weakness are nothing in comparison with those where you close your ears to the voice of the Holy Spirit as he begins to speak in the depths of your heart.

Restlessness and wounded self-love will never mend those sins that are not noticed until after they are committed. Those feelings are simply the impatience of an injured pride at seeing itself defeated. You must instead humble yourself quietly and in peace. I say "in peace" because it is not humility to repent with frustration or annoyance. You must condemn your sins, mourn over them, and turn away from them without seeking the slightest shadow of consolation from any excuse. You must see yourself covered with shame in the presence of God. But you must do all this without being bitter towards yourself or discouraged but peacefully reaping the benefits of your humiliation. Thus from the serpent himself, you extract the antidote for his venom.

Don't be surprised or discouraged by your sins. You're not more wicked than you used to be—you are actually less so—but as your wickedness decreases, your understanding of your wickedness increases, and you are thus horrified by the extent of your sin. To console yourself, you must remember that the awareness of the disease is the first step in curing it. You must not be discouraged by this awareness of your weakness. Discouragement is not a fruit of humility but of pride. Nothing is worse. If you have stumbled — or even fallen — you must get up and keep running. All of your falls are useful if they strip away your disastrous confidence in yourself without removing a humble and healthy trust in God. As Saint Theresa says, the work of grace does not always advance as orderly as the work of human nature.

Vigilantly purify your conscience, then, from daily sins. Allow no sin to dwell in your heart. Small as it may seem, it obscures the light of grace, weighs down the soul, and hinders that on-going conversation with Jesus Christ that you should be happy to cultivate. God never makes you aware of your weakness except to give you his strength. The main thing is to never act in opposition to the inner light but to instead be willing to go as far as God wants you to go.

www.ingramcontent.com/pod-product-compliance
Lightning Source LLC
Chambersburg PA
CBHW021933040426
42448CB00008B/1052